D1368446

Dedicated to
Stanislav Petrov and
Boris Yeltsin

Saving the World from
Atomic Destruction

pp. 31-32

"How can I know what I think till I see what I
      say?"

                                        -E.M. Forster

"If I waited for perfection...I would never write a
      word."

                                    -Margaret Atwood

"First you're an unknown, then you write a book
      and move up to obscurity."

                                      -Martin Meyers

"Bad things don't happen to writers; it's all
      material."

                                    -Garrison Keillor

"Easy reading is damn hard writing."

                                -Nathaniel Hawthorne

"Better to write for yourself and have no public,
      than to write for the public and have no self."

                                      -Cyril Connolly

OTHER BOOKS WRITTEN BY
James Curtis Geist

MODERN AUGUSTINIAN CONFESSION:
Memoir of a Minister, Teacher & Activist
(December 2016)

Bottom of the Food Chain:
Poems and Anecdotes *(June 2017)*

Poetry for the Kathy Lee Gifford
Child Labor Sweatshop Retirement
Village *(October 2017)*

Jimmy's Summer Beach Camping Trip
A Children's Book *(April 2018)*

Jimmy's Paper Route
A Children's Book *(April 2018)*

Jimmy's S-S-S-Summer Experience
A Children's Book *(April 2018)*

A Robot Ate My Homework:
Poems & Anecdotes for the
4th Revolution Infancy *(December 2017)*

Time Rich & Cash Poor:
Poetry and Anecdotes *(May 2018)*

Wonder Years of Teenaged Insecurity
Poetry & Anecdotes (June 2018)

Guns & Butter, Bread & Roses
Poetry & Anecdotes *(July 2018)*

Stories of the Heilige, Polter & Zeitgeist
Poetry & Anecdotes *(January 2019)*

The Presidents [1-45]
(February 2019)

Essential Geist: Volume I & II
Poetry & Anecdotes *(February 2019)*

Ragbag
Poetry & Anecdotes *(March 2019)*

My Canterbury Tale
Poetry & Anecdotes *(March 2019)*

Confession: Musings of Mischief
Poetry & Anecdotes *(April 2019)*

**Global History I, II, III & IV Notes
for Teachers** *(May 2019)*

Jimmy's Fishing Trip
A Children's Book *(May 2019)*

**United States History Notes for
Teachers** *(June 2019)*

Jimmy's Circus Trip
A Children's Book *(May 2019)*

Moonquakes
Poetry & Anecdotes *(February 2020)*

TABLE OF CONTENTS

ONE_____

Untouchable Touched	14
The Belligerent Student	15
Smoke Breaks & Candy Crush	16
Brain Fart	17
Confession 61: Paper Plates	18
Gumby & Mr. Roboto	19
Rock Band Names for Sale	20
Teacher's Lunchroom	21
Tired	22
Prank Names_1	23

TWO_____

The Empty Black Bean Shelf	26
WMHS Parking Lot 3pm	27
The Smoke Alarm	28
The Hulk	29
Confession 62: Fire Drills	31
Jersey City Lockdown 12/10/2019	32
American Healthcare is Killing Me	34
Sinus Headache	35
Happy Man	37
Prank Names_2	38

THREE_____

The World Ended 9/26/1983	40
The World Ended 1/25/1995	41
Family Enforcement	42
Help Me	43
Confession 63: Jersey City Day Laborers	44
The Committed Teacher	45
Best Doctor Visit	46
Trumper in the Checkout Line	47
Sexually Harassed at Work	48
Delaware River Route 78 Bridge	49
Prank Names_3	50

FOUR_____

Moonquakes 52

The Warehouse Fire 53

Good Master 55

The Assertive Cashier 56

Confession 64: College Kitchen Job 57

Who Are You? 58

Avoidance 59

The Dent 60

Letter to the Newark Teachers Union 62

Prank Names_4 63

FIVE_____

Creeping Out the Pilot Store Cashier 65

Hot Fudge Sunday 67

A.A. Chips on the Tombstones 68

The Werewolf Howl 69

Confession 65: School Fight 70

Teamwork 71

Annual Invasions 72

The Nod 73

Lincoln's Top Hat 75

Prank Names_5 76

SIX_____

Fun City 79

The Innocents in Jail 80

Corey Wise; Central Park Five: 1989 81

First Taste of Antisemitism 93

Confession 66: Computer Dating 94

Diner Hipsters 95

Boing Sandwich 96

Zip, Zip, Zip 97

Never Again 98

Prank Names_6 100

SECTION 1

The Untouchable Touched
[d. May 7th, 1957]

Eliot Ness
of A.T.F. and
Chicago gangster
Al Capone
arresting fame,
fought against
the evils of
alcohol making
during prohibition
days,
died at
age 54
in Coudersport P.A.,

The most
famous federal agent,
died from a
heart attack
and his
alcohol diseased
drinking ways.

The "Untouchable"
touched by
drink
he helped
raze.

The Belligerent Suspension Room Student

To the teachers he said,
"I don't care!"

To his father he said,
"I don't care!"

To the guidance counselor he said,
"I don't care!"

To the Assistant Principal he said,
"I don't care!"

To the Principal he said,
"I don't care."

To the Social Worker he said,
"I don't care!"

To the Child Study Team workers he said,
"I don't care!"

To the School Psychologist he said,
"I don't care!"

The young man was nice to me
as the suspension room coordinator.
I was lucky - he liked me.

The young man had the power
to not care because in three years
he would be buried by cancer.

Smoke Breaks and Candy Crush

In 2018,
research showed
that workers
who take smoke breaks
during work
waste 6 days
of productivity
a year.

Research also shows.
workers lose 8 hours
a week of productivity
by playing
on their cell phones
equaling 10 days
of productivity
a year.

Non-smokers
are asking
for an extra
six days of
vacation per year.

I should get
an extra 16 days
of vacation since
I neither smoke
nor own
a cell phone.

Brain Fart

Working as the Suspension Room Monitor at West Milford
    High [2018-19] I have 1050 hours to write. I write
    five books in nine months.

Working as a classroom teacher [Fall 2019], I don't have
    time to write; only for lessons, grades, teaching
    and calling parents of the troubled trouble makers.

I finally get 6 days off for the NJEA Atlantic City
    Conference and Veterans Day break to enjoy the
    process of
thinking,
writing,
editing &
revising.

It is in the process,
I find satisfaction,
joy, feelings
and gratitude.

On my first morning off, a Thursday,
I go through my black teaching satchel to
grab my Moonquakes Notes manila folder

only to realize my
folder of ideas
were left back in
my teacher desk drawer
in Jersey City.

17

Confession 61

Sometimes

I

wipe

down

my

paper

plate

and

reuse

it.

Gumby & Mr. Roboto
Circa 1990

My former college dorm neighbor becomes a teacher
in Vermont. His name was Peter, we called him
"Gumby," and his students called him Mr. W. Gumby
is a creative, humorous history teacher with his smart
aleck Long Island attitude and love for God and the
heart of a servant.

On this Spring day he teaches a lesson about robots on
the playground and asks for a volunteer that he wraps
in aluminum foil and masking tape while playing the
song "Mr. Roboto" by the rock group Styx.

Sammy volunteers and happens to suffer from
albinism. Sammy walks around in a robotic suit
of aluminum foil on this hot day, reflecting off his
robotic suit, as Mr. W. teaches his lesson to the
background music of "Mr. Roboto."

Frantically, Sammy in a non-robotic voice screams,
"Mr. W, Mr. W, I am burning up! Help!. Help!
I am on fire!" The kid who was whiter than white, was
cooking faster than the song "Hot, Hot, Hot!" by
Buster Poindexter. Several kids jumped in ripping the
aluminum foil off Sammy like a Christmas gift
whose body looked like a New Years Day Ham.

When turning a human into a robot on a warm sunny
day, it is best to avoid using students surviving from
albinism.

19

Rock Band Names for Sale A-Z

The...

Aye-Ayes	Nerveless
Bartizans	Oversexed
Chacmas	Parabolas
Derringers	Quarantined
Egg Shells	Rank-n-File
Fishmongers	Schlock
Grapples	Tedious
Hookahs	Ultimatum
Incurables	Vagabonds
Joggles	Weed
Knots	Xebecs
Lutes	Ying Yangs
Mange	Zap

Teacher's Lunch Room

West Milford High School
November 2018

Blah, blah, blah…
Does anyone watch the
Naked and Afraid TV Show?

Yea – blah, blah, blah.

Imagine trying
to survive 21 days
in the jungle naked
with all those wild
animals and insects.

I chime in,

Working in a
public school is
like being on the show
Naked and Afraid,
but
without the
naked part.

The teachers laugh
and nod in agreement as they
chew and chomp on their dinner
leftovers of meatloaf, pizza and
baked chicken legs the day
before the Thanksgiving break.

Tired

Damn am I tired!

No rest for the cherry; I mean
no rest for the cheery; I mean
no rest for the leery.
Damn am I tired!

No rest for the query; I mean
no rest for the smeary; I mean
no rest for the Kashmiri.
Damn am I tired!

No rest for the thirty; I mean
no rest for the dreary; I mean
no rest for the teary.
Damn am I tired!

No rest for THE WEARY!

TIRED!
TiReD!
TireD!
Tir_____zzzzzzzzzzz...

Prank Names #1

Adam Bomb

Barbie Dahl

Carrie Oakey

Fran Tick

Hammond Eggs

Igor Beever

Juan Manband

Lee King

Mark Z. Spot

SECTION 2

Empty Black Bean Shelf

My Filipina wife loves black beans.
In early May we stop by the Shoprite,
but the all the bags of black beans are gone.
There are lentils, favas, navies and pintos,
but no black beans.

My wife says, "Ahhhh,
the Mexicans bought
all the black beans.

Was the comment racist?
It was a few days before
the Cinco de Mayo celebration.

In mid-March,
at the Shoprite,   I go to
the vinegar aisle,
but it is all gone.

I look at Helen and say,
"The Irish bought out
all the vinegar."

Was my comment racist?
It is a few days before
St. Patrick's Day
cabbaged beef
was going to be cooked
and consumed.

West Milford High School Parking Lot @ 3pm

Honk, honk!

VROOM, VROOM.....

Clank, clank, clank.....

Screeeeeehhhh!

Pb-pb-pb-b-b-b-b

Beep, Beep!

Tick, tick, tick, tick, tick.....

Rumble-rumble-rumble-sputter

VaRoom, VaRoom!

Honk, honk!

Eeeeeergh!

Pop-pop-pop-pop-pop

Vroom, vroom, VROOM!

VaRoom, Varoom_ga-ga-ga-ga-ga.....

Beep, beep!

27

The Smoke Alarm

My wife works the second shift and after her snack and shower, crawls into the bed to put her cold body against mine at the 11:45pm hour. It like having cold water dumped on you during a warm shower.

The smoke alarm goes off 10 minutes later with the deafening sound of "EH – EH - EH – EH – EH!

The wife wakes up in a panic. "Jim, what is that?" I jump out of bed, smell no smoke, see no fire, and grab a newspaper waving it back and forth below the smoke alarm until the alarm stops. The alarm is electric, so it is not like I can pull the batteries out.

The alarm stops. My heart is pounding. My brow is sweating. It will be some time before I will be able to fall into a deep sleep again.

I lean on the stairway balcony trying to figure out why this alarm went off. I smell camp fire smoke. It is wafting off of my jeans and sweatshirt on the balcony just below the fire alarm.

I did enjoy a campfire that evening after dinner. I take the campfire infused clothing, and throw them on the outside deck.

Problem solved.

The Hulk

Vincent is a student who use to stop by the Suspension
  room daily at the end of the school day to say hello.
  He was high on the autism spectrum, and with his
  great attitude, was going to do well in life.

He was a Special Education student who worked at
  McDonalds, was on the wrestling team and went to
  the Prom with his date.   He was a gentleman and I
  looked forward to our daily conversations. Vinny was
  a highlight of my 2018-19 school year.

On the last day of school, in a room of seven students in the
  "Refocusing Center," Vincent stormed in the room
  with the A.P. right behind him.

A mini-riot broke among some excited seniors who were
  graduating. Of course, the security cameras caught all
  of the trouble-makers.

*You spit on the floor, and now you will not walk in the
  graduation ceremony!*

Vinny grabbed a desk, lifted it up and threw it on the
  ground.

*And now you are not allowed to attend the graduation
  ceremony!*

29

Vinny grabbed another desk, picked it up and threw it on the ground.

Follow me, I now have to call the police.

All I could think was, "This kid made it through his senior year, and now at the 1 yard line and 99/100 of the way to graduation, lost some control.

At the end of the day, when cooler heads prevailed, the A.P. walked in with Vinny and said, *Vinny wants to talk with you.*

"Mr. Geist, I am embarrassed how I acted in front of you. It was inappropriate, and I don't want you remembering me this way. I want to make sure my slate with you is clean."

He leaned over and with tears in his eyes, gave me a big hug. "Please don't think less of me. I have high regard for you."

Vinny always had my respect, but even more so that he was able to admit mistakes and apologize for them.

Vinny walked graduation the next day and is a Facebook friend of mine.

Confession 62

Fire Drills

As a teacher
when I had
no students
in class,
I hid
in my room
at least
4-5 times
during the
monthly
fire drill;

I was
working
on
school work
or
the weather
was
cold
or
inclement.

Jersey City Lockdown 12/10/2019

I begin working at METs Charter School – Jersey City Campus – in mid-September of 2019.

My commute to work is one hour but two hours home in bumper to bumper traffic. In the morning I drive around looking for a parking spot with alternative street parking. I witness stray cats, raccoons, and skunks walking the streets of a city next to the Hudson River across from the Manhattan skyline.

As I stroll to school, I pass the corner where two workers sitting in their van smoking their daily chronic jay bone. While I do not partake, I enjoy the smell.

I pass joggers, the corner bodega, the home with glazed green clay pots on the stairwell, the Jeep with the "Wander Forever" sticker on the back window and the white cat who greets me two to three times a week when I say, "Good morning puss, puss."

On the morning of clear skies and a full moon, our school will have a "Lock Down" announced at 2:30pm.

Since the Columbine High School Shooting in 1999, part of the monthly school schedules have been practicing "Lock Downs," where doors are locked, and no one is allowed out of the classroom or into the schools until the "all clear" has been announced.

The practice drills usually last 3-4 minutes, but on January 10th of 2019, no "all clear" is announced.

Students begin getting antsy at 2:55pm, since dismissal takes place at 2:57pm. The "all clear is not announced at 2:57pm, or 3:30pm, or 4pm, and students want to leave. I go on the computer and see if the school has posted the following warning: "The Jersey City police calling for a lockdown of all Jersey City schools until further notice."

By 5:30pm, the internet has articles posted by all the local television stations that there has been a gun fight for several hours in downtown Jersey City. At 5:55pm, it is announced one police officer, two store owners a store customer and the shooter couple have been shot and killed.

The killers turn out to be Black Hebrews who do not like Hebrews who are not Black Hebrews; it is deemed a "hate crime."

The class becomes quiet after learning the news. At 6pm, the students are dismissed.

Not all lockdowns are for practice. I think, if this had to happen, I wish it had been on a Professional Development Day, because those meetings are
B-O-R-I-N-G!!!

American Healthcare is Killing Me

My first net paycheck at Mets Charter School (2019) is $2400. I work on my budget and figure out I will be able to pay my bills, take out my wife once a month for a movie and dinner, and have $500 extra left over to pay off some debt, pay some principle off the mortgage and squirrel enough away to not have to house paint or teach summer school in July or August.

My next check is $2150, $250 less or $500 less a month. They union rep tells me $500 comes out a month to pay for my health insurance.

DAMN!

This is a way NJ Governor Christie has punished teachers for being mostly Democrats by increasing teacher healthcare payments (not cops or firemen).

The American Healthcare system is killing me (financially). Single payer universal healthcare is so complicated, that only 31 of 32 first world countries are able to pull it off.

I can't believe I will spend another summer house painting to meet my monthly budge nut. When will I be able to escape ladders, scraping, sanding, priming and finish coating?

Damn!

I spit on the ground every time I hear Governor Fattie's name.

Sinus Headache
January 2020

3 am: splitting sinus headache

3:01 am: a few curse words

3:04 am: Sudafed – watch Forensic Files on TV

3:20 am: left side of head beginning to clear

3:21 am: Vicks Vapor Rub on chest and nostrils

4:29 am: take "breathe-easy" strip off the nose

4:30 am: hot shower

4:35 am: left side of head 90% cleared

4:40 am: cough drops

5 am: right side of head still hurting

5:30 am: leave for work on this 16 degree day

5:45 am   take two Excedrin pills

6 am: most of congestion gone

6:45 am: Ahhhhhh - RELIEF!

6:46 am: Amen, Hallelujah!

The Happy Man

School Nurse Frank was always smiling.
If you asked him how he was doing, with
a great big syrupy smile would boom
"Fantastic!" or "Wonderful!" or "The
Best!" It was disconcerting to me to see
someone so happy.

He was smiling when it was sunny, raining,
warm or cold. He was smiling whether it
was Monday, Friday or any day in
between.   Was School Nurse Frank that
happy or covering his Carl Jungian
shadow of a hidden sad life?

Perhaps Nurse Frank was a millionaire; or
had the most beautiful, perfect and
submissive girlfriend, or belonged to the
"Shiny-Happy-People" cult.   Perhaps he
was a serial killer trying to throw the cops
off his scent. Medical cannabis perhaps?

It was a strange day when I saw Nurse
Frank not smiling. In fact, he looked
depressed, scared and panicked. In that
moment I knew School Nurse Frank
belonged to the human race that trod, trod,
trods in the face of difficulties, depression
and desperation.

Neither School Nurse Frank nor the other teachers were smiling on that fateful Tuesday after receiving an e-mail from the Superintendent the evening before (2/5/20) stating the Education Department of New Jersey was closing down our school.

Many expressed "concern for the children," I said, "The children do not have to wory about paying a mortgage."

In the end, all working people are only two paychecks away from the road to homelessness - you can live in your home 6 months without paying the mortgage before the Sheriff shows up to kick you out of your foreclosed home.

Can you spell "eviction?"

The only thing that made me happy that day was seeing Nurse Frank behaving the way a normal human should respond to devastating news.

Prank Names #2

Al E. Gator

Bea Sting

Chris Mass

Dan Druff

Frank Furter

Harry Butz

Ima Hogg

Justyn Tyme

Lou Natic

Mary Wana

SECTION 3

The World Ended 9/26/83

September 26th, 1983:
The Soviet early warning satellite system
at the Serpukhove-15 bunker
outside of Moscow reported that
U.S. intercontinental ballistic missiles
were heading to the Soviet Union.

The Soviets
responded in kind,
and the U.S.
and U.S.S.R.
were destroyed in
a nuclear holocaust.

THE END

Post-Script:
Lieutenant colonel of the Soviet Air Defense Forces
Stanislav Petrov suspected the system was malfunctioning
and convinced his superiors.
He argued if the U.S. was going to attack pre-emptively, it
would do so with more than just five missiles.
Petrov thought it best to wait for ground radar confirmation
before launching a counter-attack.

Sometimes computer systems mistake
sun reflections off the clouds
for a nuclear missile.

Stanislav Petrov
is the man who saved the world.

The World Ended 1/25/1995

January 25th, 1995:
The Russian early warning satellite system
reported that an American first strike or
U.S. intercontinental ballistic missiles
were heading to Russia.

Boris Yeltsin
responded in kind,
and the U.S.
and Russia
were destroyed in
a nuclear holocaust.

THE END

Post-Script:
President Boris Yeltsin was given a suitcase with
instructions for launching the nuclear strike at the U.S.
Yeltsin declined to launch the counterstrike.

Sometimes a computer systems mistake
joint Norwegian-U.S. northern lights research rockets
for nuclear missiles.

<u>Boris Yeltsin</u>
is the man who saved the world.

Family Enforcement

circa 2001

My
five year
old nephew is sitting
in an inflatable plastic lounge chair bouncing up
and down. Nan says, "Jordan, stop bouncing in the chair."

He
looks at
her and with an
impish smile, begins bouncing
again. Uncle Jim walks over, and kicks the chair and
says, "When Nana tells you to do something, you listen."

The
fear on
his face was as
if a grizzly bear was about to maul him alive.

I
have had
plenty of times in
my life when I needed a family member
to set me straight, and I am know Jordan will pass it on to
the next generation when he/she needs to be
taught a lesson about
"respecting the
elders."

Help Me

I sat on my deck
that late Spring afternoon
approximately 6 pm
when a hawk flew by me
through the
eight foot canyon
between my home
and the home of
neighbor Richie.

I could have sworn
I heard "Help me!"
as the large mouse
or small rat dangling
in crucifix position with
bird of prey talons
through the left
and right shoulders
swooped and sailed past me
with a look of desperation
and brutal acceptance
of imminent death
making eye contact me.

The sacrifice of the
carnivorous animal kingdom
about to be partaken
in the circle of life.

Confession 63

Jersey City Day Laborers
circa the winter of 2019

Twice a month during
the work day,
I treat myself to a
$1 McDonald's coffee
and Egg McMuffin.

When Micky D's
runs the
$1 special for a
second sandwich

I buy one
and give it to
the homeless guy
on the corner or one
of the undocumented
day laborers standing
by the mall entryway.

It is it part
of my tithe and
the pay off
is the grateful
smile on s
human mug.

The Committed Teacher

The High School teacher, aged 72, confided in me,
"I will be working until I am 76."

"Wow, you must really be committed to your craft!"

The septuagenarian pedagogue replied,
"I emigrated to this country late in my life.
I must work until age 76 to get my
Social Security 40 quarters (10 years) to
be eligible for Social Security and Medicare.

His commitment was to
getting healthcare and
retirement income was
equal to investing in
the future of teens.

I identify!

When I turn 65,
I plan on collecting
Social Security and
Medicare.
50% of the people
I know died,
before age 65!

Being a pensioner is not
for wussies or those who
are not able to live past age 65.

45

The Best Doctor's Visit
Circa 2019

I was having pain in my groin area –
pain similar to the hernia pain I felt
30 years earlier when I was in college.

I went to see a urologist and
the doctor asked me how old I was.

I am 54 years old.

When were you born?

March 2nd, 1966.

Mr. Geist - you are 53 years old.

What?!?! Are you sure?

I was born in February of 1965, and I am 54.
YOU….are…..53.

Interesting.
I have always preferred
my birthdate falling on
an even number over
an odd number.

Somewhere between age 50 and 53,
I mixed up my true age.
The doctor gave me an extra year of life and
THAT is a great Doctor's visit!

Trumper in the Checkout Line

B.J.'s Store; Riverdale NJ – 2-8-20 (a.m.)

As I am scanning granola bars, Lance's crackers and my
Bubba Burgers at the self check out line with my wife at
my side, I notice a Trumper across from me.

She is a woman in her late 60s, with dark curly hair, her
MAGA hat on, blue jeans and a black shirt with an
American flag and soaring eagle on it.

The B.J.'s roaming cashier supervisor walks over to ask
the Trumper would like help. Ms. Trumper with disgust on
her face, looks at the worker, an African American female
and says, "I don't need any help!   I really don't need help.
I don't nee YOUR help" in a dismissive and rude manner.

The supervisor walks away to help others. I really hate
bullies and I hate to see anyone get bullied. As we begin
our exit, I walk over the supervisor and say, "I am really
sorry. I want to apologize."

The Supervisor looks at me like, "What is this honky
talking about?" I say, "I sometimes hate white people
too." The supervisor puts her hand on my shoulder, and
laughs so hard, she buckles over and the reading glasses on
the top of her head fall to the ground.

She says to me, "Mister, you made my day!"   Wife Helen
asks me what I said to make the B.J.'s worker laugh so
hard.

Sexually Harassed at Work
Winter 2019

My wife is a certified home health aide
at an assisted living facility. She
sometimes helps the infirmed clients take
showers or baths.

She helped bathe an older gentleman and
he asked the wife to also wash his penis
and to dry it off.

The wife said, "I will help bathe you, but I
am not washing or drying your penis! You
can do it yourself Peter." The old man,
with erect penis says, "You can touch it.
No one else has touched it in years."

The wife files a sexual harassment
complaint with her boss, and the
gentleman admits to saying what the
wife had written up.

I told the wife, "If the old man had thrown
in an extra $20 for private area washing, it
would have been fine with me. That $13.50
an hour job needs to be supplemented
somehow.

48

Delaware River Bridge on Route 78

The wife and I cross the Delaware River Bridge on Route 78 from New Jersey into Pennsylvania at least 18-22 times a year visiting family and friends.

As the automobile starts motoring across the bridge, the driver and riders will pass at five light poles attached to the outside parapets of the concrete bridge.

The state line runs in the middle of the river, and as the wife and I drive unto the bridge, we play a fun game where we chant, "New Jersey, New Jersey, New Jersey" and then "Pennsylvania when we see the "0" on the green sign posted on the middle pole (the third light pole) on the bridge. We do the opposite chant when we cross from Pennsylvania back into New Jersey.

As you enter Pennsylvania, there is a large blue metal sign, 25 feet by 20 feet that says, **"Welcome to Pennsylvania! Pursue your happiness!"**

As you enter New Jersey, there is a green metal sign 6 feet by 4 feet that has the state outline on a stamp, that says in small letters, **"Welcome to New Jersey!"** The New Jersey welcoming sign actually looks as big as a U.S. stamp.

It seems to me, the state Pennsylvania does a much better job welcoming motorist alumni and visitors than the state New Jersey. The New Jersey entry sign might as well say, *"Welcome to New Jersey - meh."*

Prank Names #3

Al Koholic

Beau Vine

Chris P. Bacon

Dick Tater

Cary Oakie

Helen Back

Jacques Strappe

Lou Sirr

Miya Buttreeks

SECTION 4

Moonquakes

When I think of the moon, I think of craters, moon rocks, the Apollo Flights from 1969 to 1977, the man in the moon, the dark side of the moon and the earthly satellite that serves as a friend to insomniacs.

I think of the celestial object rotating around Mother Earth producing ocean tides, body tides, slight lengthening of the day and werewolves evolving when the moon is full, shiny and the owl can be heard hooting in the woods.

In 2019 I learn the moon experiences quakes; a concept fills me with surprise, intrigue and wonder. A moonquake is the lunar equivalent of an earthquake.

Earthquakes are caused by volcanic eruptions, meteor impacts, oil extraction, but mostly by the constantly moving 20 plates releasing stress and energy that moving through the earth as seismic waves.

Moonquakes twitch and tremble, vibrate and rumble, pulsate and fluctuate, heaving and jerking, shivering and writhing; and while moonquakes are weaker than earthquakes, reaching magnitudes of 5.5.

What does this mean? It means the first humans to settle on earth will need quake-proof housing, but more importantly, it gives my book of poetry and anecdotes a crisp title and cool looking book cover.

Warehouse Fire by Fountain Park
Circa 1977

In the Allentown Pennsylvania Morning Call newspaper dated February 8th of 1977, is a picture of my Uncle Fritz helping tuck the blanket over in an injured fireman in an ambulance stretcher. The fire took place across the street from Fountain Park in a warehouse at the corner of Lawrence (now M.L.K. Blvd) and South Jefferson Streets.

I kept this article in my files for over 42 years. I framed the article and gave it to my Uncle Fritz in 2019. Before giving him the article, I show my father the newspaper picture. My father William says, "I was at that fire as well!" Six Allentown Firemen are injured while fighting this particular fire.

In 1977, Dad stopped by Nana Geist's, and she said, "Bill, there is a fire at the warehouse, and Fritz is up there." Dad walks up the hill to check out the action and sees a fireman put a ladder against a brick wall where the roof is on fire.

Dad thinks to himself, "That wall cannot be too sturdy to put a ladder against." No sooner than the thought finishes, and the wall collapses covering the fireman with bricks and fire.

Dad flags down a fireman at the other end of the building, and the fireman says "Hey buddy, let us do our job." Dad says, "You have fireman injured, covered in bricks and fire!"

The fireman runs over, finds his fire fighting comrade, and calls Dad over saying, "Grab him by the pants and we will pull him out." They pull the injured fireman out and he is put on the ambulance for his ride to the hospital.

Forty two years later, I ask Uncle Fritz if he remembers Dad being at the fire and he says "I don't." Dad says to me, "Can you imagine that? I helped to save the life of a fireman, get no mention in the article, but Uncle Fritz gets his picture in the paper."

Good Master

In 2002 I dated a
Chinese woman named Huan.
It was pronounced Juan,
but I called her
Huuuuuu-aaaaaaan.
She did not seem to mind.

Huan was tall,
liked badminton and
ball room dancing.
From her I learned
how to say "thank-you"
in Chinese - "Shea-shea"

I once had guests over
to my Queens apartment
and Huan said,
"Jim is a good master."
It felt weird because slavery
had been illegal for over 130 years,
moreover,
I had been the NYC director of the
American Anti-Slavery Group
from 1996-2002.

By "master,"
Huan really meant
teacher.

THE ASSERTIVE CASHIER

Setting: Shoprite Express Lane – 15 or less items.

This is the express lane.

I understand.

THIS [pregnant pause], *is the express lane.*

Yup.

This IS the express lane SIR!

Which I why I am standing here Mam.

Hairy eyeball look from the cashier.
Returned slightly annoyed look
from this customer.

*It looks like you have more than
15 items in your cart.*

**Maam, I have 13 items in this cart,
thus, the express lane.**

*Oh. It looks like you have
more than 15 items in your cart.*

I admired her due diligence.
There are too many
express lane barbarians
with grocery carts filled to the brim.

56

Confession 64

Evangelical College Kitchen Cleaning Job
1988

When I
was a
college student,
I mopped
the college
kitchen floor
twice a week
from 9-11pm.

More than
the meager
minimum wages,
I worked
the kitchen
to nab snacks
because I was
so hungry
at times.

Who Are You?

I am a
Son
Brother
Grandson
Husband
Friend
Student
Teacher
Human Rights Activist
Political Animal
Hoopster
Fisherman
Hunter
Homeowner
Landscaper.

That is not who you are.
That is what you do.

Who are you?

* * *

I am the Walrus....

Ku-Ku-Ka-Chu.

Avoidance

Alcohol	Reading
Food	Music
Chocolate	Television
Sugar	Fantasizing
Coffee	Web Surfing
Romance	Workaholism
Sex	Excitement
Movies	Approval

Some of the ways I avoid
responsibility and
processing feelings

The Dent

Spring of 2019

I buy a 2014 black Ford C-Max Hybrid
(39 mpg) the winter of 2018.

On a Saturday Spring after completing my
morning food shopping errand to Shoprite,
I notice a dent on my driver's side door.

Did it happen Friday
at the parking lot
of West Milford High School
or Saturday morning
at the Shoprite parking lot?

The following Saturday
on my food shopping pilgrimage,
after parking the C-Max,
I see an old lady
swinging her car into a
180 degree circle
to pull into a parking spot.
As she does so,
she scrapes and scratches
the driver's side door
of a parked vehicle.

Granny with the
wire-rim eye-glasses
and blue hair
looks around
to see if there are
any witnesses,
and slowly
pulls away to park
to the opposite end
of the parking lot.

I am too busy
to be snitching
and filling out
police reports
on this glorious
Saturday Spring
    morning.

*Is this the person
who dented my car
last week?*

How will she sleep tonight?

*Will she go to Confession at
Queen of Peace Church
this week?*

Newark Teachers Union Letter

February 5, 2020

Dear N.T.U. President,

Based on the articles I read in the morning papers, the Newark Teachers Union supported the Newark School Superintendent's proposal of closing four charter schools in Newark. I understand why public schools and unions would be against charter schools with no union affiliation.

Any argument that is controversial, is controversial because it has good arguments on both sides. I work at, METS Charter School (Jersey City Campus), <u>that does have union representation</u> via the *New Jersey Education Association.*

<u>Unions are part of the solution of improving charter schools.</u> **Solidarity means showing support for your fellow union brother and sisters, especially in the pedagogical field.**

The next time you choose to close down a charter school in Newark, the union should focus on the schools without union representation. *This is not Solidarity! This is throwing your fellow union brothers and sisters under the bus. It is called "eating your own."*

When a union lose one member, it loses power. I am sorely disappointed and betrayed by the leadership of the Newark Teachers Union.

Jim Geist

Jim Geist

Mets Charter School   cc: NJEA President

Crank Names #4

Al Luminum

Bill Bored

Collin Sick

Ella Mentry

Jerry Mander

Homer Sexual

Otto Matik

Penny Less

Seymour Butz

Urika Garlic

SECTION 5

Creeping Out the Pilot Gas Station Cashier

Every time Helen and I drive to Pennsylvania to visit the folks, we stop by the Pilot Gas Station and Truck Stop in Hampton New Jersey to get a cup of coffee or to use the rest room and/or fill up with gasoline. The gas pump guys are friendly, cordial and always willing to wash your windshields – it is like taking a trip back in time, and I am grateful for it.

As I walk in on this April Saturday, the female cashier looks just like my cousin Becky. I stare at her with a quizzical look thinking, "Why would Cousin Becky take a job so far away from Allentown?" I can see the cashier looking at me as I look at her looking at me and I rush off to the bathroom.

On the way out of the bathroom, I walk up to the woman and apologize and explained why I had stared at her. Her name was Brittany, and she thanked me for the explanation saying, "It did creep me out a little." I say, "My apologies Brittany."

Many criminologists believe one of the best jobs for a serial killer is to be a truck driver, where you cross state lines frequently. I can understand why Brittany, the truck stop cashier, became uncomfortable when she thought I peering and leering at her. It is also why I apologized to her to not ruin her day.

The Ted Bundy killings across state lines made it difficult for police agencies to capture him, the F.B.I. created VICAP [the Violent Criminal Apprehension Program] to help connect the dots with serial killers. For those who kill in different cities, or counties in a state, or across state lines, it is often difficult tracking down and capturing such killers.

Canada picked up on our VICAP program, only they require all Canadian police agencies to send all crime scene reports to their central agency. It is a shame that it is not mandatory for the police in the U.S. to send all said reports to the F.B.I. so we can better track and capture these serial killer freaks.

66

Hot Fudge Sunday

Whenever
I
order a
hot fudge
Sunday
over a
drive-thru
ordering
booth,
I
ALWAYS
ask
for
peanuts
with
it.

I
always
hope
the
cashier
hears
the
word
peanuts,
not
penis.

A.A. Chips on the Tombstones
circa the Winter of 2014

As I looked at the Tombstones in the East Dorset
Vermont Cemetery of William G. Wilson [1895-1971]
and Lois B. Wilson [1891-1988], I notice
approximately 100 plus "chips" or A.A. tokens on the
tombstone of Bill W., and half a dozen on the
tombstone of his wife Lois.

Bill W. is the founding member of Alcoholics
Anonymous, and his wife Lois is known as the First
Lady of Al-anon, a 12 step group for family and
friends of alcoholics. While she was not an alcoholic,
she is called the co-founder of A.A.

The placing of the sobriety chips on a tombstone is a
sign of visitation and respect for the deceased.
Sobriety chips are given out for the 1st, 2nd, 3rd, 6th and
9th months in your first year of sobriety. After that,
sobriety tokens are given out for yearly anniversaries.

 While I do not identify as an alcoholic, I am grateful
for all the 12 step programs that have been birthed out
of the A.A. program. It upset me there were so few
coins on the tombstone of Lois.

I moved half of the coins from Bill's tombstone to
hers. I said, "Lois, this is for all the distress and
heart-ache Bill put you through before his recovery.
Thank-you for all you done for me and for the
recovering codependents of the world.

68

West Milford NJ Werewolf Howl

As a sophomore in high school circa 1981,
I watch the movie
American Werewolf in London.
The two American boys hiking
in the farmlands of England are warned to
"Stay off the moors on the night of a full moon."

As they walk the moors on the full moon lit evening,
an eerie echoing howling can be heard
in the distance getting closer and closer.
Baaaaaa-oooooohhh! BAAAAAAA-OOOOOOHH!
The hair on the back of my neck
        stands.

In the past 35 years,
when the movie is shown on television,
even with the dated visual effects,
and I hear THAT howl,
the hair on the back of my neck
        still stands.

As I sit on my back deck in the evenings star-gazing,
my neighbor's dog up the hillside gives out
the same creepy howl of the werewolf in the moors
in the movie American Werewolf in London.

Even though I know it is only a movie,
my neighbor's dog howling makes
the hair on the back of my neck
        stand.

Confession 65
Student Fight

As a
student fight
broke out
in the hallway
between
periods 3-4,
a petite
English teacher
with blond hair
hit me in the arm
and screeched,
"Get in there!
Break it up!"

I looked
at her and
wanted to say,

Sister,
in the age of
equal rights,
be my guest.
Step into the middle
of the crazed
student frenzy
and earn your
equal pay!

70

Teamwork

A memory I cherish of
Mom and Dad
circa 1983 took place
at the kitchen table of
512 College Drive in Allentown Pa.

Mom was studying to become a
Registered Nurse.

As Mom read,
wrote notes and
hand wrote her paper,
Dad, an assembly line U.A.W.
Mack Truck assembly line worker,
took her notes with
reading glasses balanced on his nose
typing the paper
rat-a-tat-tat,
using his index fingers
on the Smith & Corona Manual Typewriter
Nana & Grandpa Short gave Mom.

Dad's typing
was an
act of love
shown in a practical way.

T-E-A-M-W-O-R-K!

The Annual Invasions

In the Spring and mid-Winter I will see dark rice grains on the stove and/or hear the scurrying of little feet in the attic or bedroom walls. A container of crushed corn is in the work room I use to feed the wild turkeys that roost behind my rural home.

Mouse One: On this night, a small mouse has fallen in the open 5 gallon Home Depot orange bucket and cannot jump out. I place a trap with peanut-butter and the next morning the mouse is deceased in the trap.

Mouse Two: I put out traps on the first floor work room and in the kitchen approximately 7pm; in the time of the Winter Sun setting at 4:30pm. Snap!
As of 8pm, I have vermin number 2.

Mouse Three: In the morning, is mouse number 3 with his feet sticking up in the air.

Mice 4-7: Over the next three days, the traps harvest four more mice. Who am I kidding? Harvested? Four vermin mice have been killed.

Don't let those cute furry faces with big round brown eyes fool you. Mice and rats carried the fleas infected with Bubonic Plague killing an estimated 50 million humans during the Middle Ages!

I put the traps away until the next home invasion.

The Nod

circa the Spring of 2003

In the summer of 2003, as I
exited the Shoprite Food Store
in Ramapo New Jersey,
strolling towards my 1996 green
Jeep Sport, donning my
orange, black and white
Philadelphia Flyers jersey,
a blond-headed man
sauntered towards me.

It is none other than
the native Oklahoman and
quarterback of the New York Giants
(1979-1993), Phil Simms.

Simms led the Giants to
Superbowl victories in 1986
(against the Broncos) and
in 1991 (against the Bills).

We made eye contact on the
Shoprite parking macadam,
and in his mind's eye,
I could see Simms thinking,

"I hope this is not a crazy
Philadelphia Eagles fan who is
going to make a smart-ass
comment to me."

Knowing how much Phil Simms
gets badgered in public,
I nodded at him in solidarity
of respect for his privacy.

Phil nodded back
to me as if to say, "
Thanks Philadelphia
sports fan
for not being
a star -f___ker."

Lincoln's Silk Top Hat
April of 2019

My parents visit nephew Jordan, aged 24, at his new flat in Washington D.C. He has been working at the Pentagon, but will be taking on a new job in the near future elsewhere.

While Jordan gives the folks the tour of Washington D.C., they tour the Museum of American History. Dad walks up to a glass booth with a silk top hat, and it turns out to be the hat 6'4" President Lincoln wore the night he was killed at Ford Theater. Dad gets emotional looking at this piece of history.

Helen and I visit Aunt Sandy and her dog, and I tell her the story about Mom, Dad and Jordan and Lincoln's hat. She says, "My maiden name is Spangler, and I am related to Edmund Spangler, a carpenter and stagehand at the Ford Theater who was part of the seven person conspiracy that assassinated Lincoln on April 14th of 1865. I am not proud of it, but it part of my family history."

Helen and I listen to Mom and Dad's Lincoln hat story on a Saturday night. Helen and I listen Aunt Sandy's story the following Sunday morning.

It was an unusual confluence of events indeed.

Prank Names #5

Ann Jyna

Bud Wiser

Dinah Mite

Eric Tyle

Ginger Vitis

Hy Gene

Ray Ling

Pete Zaria

Sue E. Side

Val Crow

SECTION 6

FUN CITY [1970's-1980's]

1970's Bankruptcy
Police Corruption - Serpico
Twin Towers
Saturday Night Fever
The Black Out
Crime, Drugs, Gangs, Crack, AIDS
The Warriors Movie
I Love NY campaign
Yankees (77,78) Mets (86) Giants (87)
Bronx on Fire
Guardian Angels
Mayor Ed Koch
Sanitation & MTA strikes
Howard Beach Race Riots
Rapper's Delight & Run DMC
John Lennon shot
Late Night with David Letterman
Subway Vigilante Bernhard Goetz
Son of Sam, Rev. Al Sharpton
Gambino Boss Castellano shot at Steak House
Curtis Sliwa shot by Gotti connections
Trump fixes Wollman Rink
Preppie Murder Central Park
Aids Quilt Central Park
Parking Ticket Vehicle Impounds
Tomkin's Square Riot
Cosby/Seinfeld
Central Park Jogger Attacked
So fun it is named twice:
New York NewYork.

79

The Innocents in Jail

Research
Shows
4%
of the
incarcerated
are
innocent.

That
comes
to 90,000
wrongly
imprisoned
Americans.
The
Shawshank
Redemption
Movie
is
the
scariest
horror
movie
to
me.

Corey Wise of the Central Park Five circa 1989

1,2,3,4,5,6,7,8,9,10,11,12,13,14,15,16,17,18,19,20,21,22,23,24,
25,26,27,28,29,30,31,32,33,34,35,36,37,38,39,40,41,42,43,44,
45,46,47,48,49,50,51,52,53,54,55,56,57,58,59,60,61,62,63,64,
65,66,67,68,69,70,71,72,73,74,75,76,77,78,79,80,81,82,83,84
,85,86,87,88,89,90,91,92,93,94,95,95,96,97,98,99,100,101,102,
103,104,105,106,107,108,109,110,111,112,113,114,115,116,
117,118,119,120,121,122,123,124,125,126,127,128,129,130,
131,132,133,134,135,136,137,138,139,140,141,142,143,144,
145,146,147,148,149,150,151,152,153,154,155,156,157,158,
159,160,161,162,163,164,165,166,167,168,169,170,171,172,
173,174,175,176,177,178,179,180,181,182,183,184,185,186,
187,188,189,190,191,192,193,194,195,196,197,198,199,200,
201,202,203,204,205,206,207,208,209,210,211,212,213,214,
215,216,217,218,219,220,221,222,223,224,225,226,227,228,
229,230,231,232,233,234,235,236,237,238,239,240,241,242,
243,244,245,246,247,248,249,250,251,252,253,254,255,256,
257,258,259,260,261,262,263,264,265,266,267,268,269,270,
271,272,273,274,275,276,277,278,279,280,281,282,283,284,
285,286,287,288,289,290,291,292,293,294,295,296,297,298,
299,300,301,302,303,304,305,306,307,308,309,310,311,312,
313,314,315,316,317,318,319,320,321,322,323,324,325,326,
327,328,329,330,331,332,333,334,335,336,337,338,339,340,
341,342,343,344,345,346,347,348,349,350,351,252,353,354,
355,356,357,358,359,360,361,362,363,364,365...

1,2,3,4,5,6,7,8,9,10,11,12,13,14,15,16,17,18,19,20,21,22,23,24,
25,26,27,28,29,30,31,32,33,34,35,36,37,38,39,40,41,42,43,44,
45,46,47,48,49,50,51,52,53,54,55,56,57,58,59,60,61,62,63,64,
65,66,67,68,69,70,71,72,73,74,75,76,77,78,79,80,81,82,83,84
,85,86,87,88,89,90,91,92,93,94,95,95,96,97,98,99,100,101,102,
103,104,105,106,107,108,109,110,111,112,113,114,115,116,
117,118,119,120,121,122,123,124,125,126,127,128,129,130,

131,132,133,134,135,136,137,138,139,140,141,142,143,144,
145,146,147,148,149,150,151,152,153,154,155,156,157,158,
159,160,161,162,163,164,165,166,167,168,169,170,171,172,
173,174,175,176,177,178,179,180,181,182,183,184,185,186,
187,188,189,190,191,192,193,194,195,196,197,198,199,200,
201,202,203,204,205,206,207,208,209,210,211,212,213,214,
215,216,217,218,219,220,221,222,223,224,225,226,227,228,
229,230,231,232,233,234,235,236,237,238,239,240,241,242,
243,244,245,246,247,248,249,250,251,252,253,254,255,256,
257,258,259,260,261,262,263,264,265,266,267,268,269,270,
271,272,273,274,275,276,277,278,279,280,281,282,283,284,
285,286,287,288,289,290,291,292,293,294,295,296,297,298,
299,300,301,302,303,304,305,306,307,308,309,310,311,312,
313,314,315,316,317,318,319,320,321,322,323,324,325,326,
327,328,329,330,331,332,333,334,335,336,337,338,339,340,
341,342,343,344,345,346,347,348,349,350,351,252,353,354,
355,356,357,358,359,360,361,362,363,364,365…

1,2,3,4,5,6,7,8,9,10,11,12,13,14,15,16,17,18,19,20,21,22,23,24,
25,26,27,28,29,30,31,32,33,34,35,36,37,38,39,40,41,42,43,44,
45,46,47,48,49,50,51,52,53,54,55,56,57,58,59,60,61,62,63,64,
65,66,67,68,69,70,71,72,73,74,75,76,77,78,79,80,81,82,83,84
,85,86,87,88,89,90,91,92,93,94,95,95,96,97,98,99,100,101,102,
103,104,105,106,107,108,109,110,111,112,113,114,115,116,
117,118,119,120,121,122,123,124,125,126,127,128,129,130,
131,132,133,134,135,136,137,138,139,140,141,142,143,144,
145,146,147,148,149,150,151,152,153,154,155,156,157,158,
159,160,161,162,163,164,165,166,167,168,169,170,171,172,
173,174,175,176,177,178,179,180,181,182,183,184,185,186,
187,188,189,190,191,192,193,194,195,196,197,198,199,200,
201,202,203,204,205,206,207,208,209,210,211,212,213,214,
215,216,217,218,219,220,221,222,223,224,225,226,227,228,
229,230,231,232,233,234,235,236,237,238,239,240,241,242,
243,244,245,246,247,248,249,250,251,252,253,254,255,256,

257,258,259,260,261,262,263,264,265,266,267,268,269,270,
271,272,273,274,275,276,277,278,279,280,281,282,283,284,
285,286,287,288,289,290,291,292,293,294,295,296,297,298,
299,300,301,302,303,304,305,306,307,308,309,310,311,312,
313,314,315,316,317,318,319,320,321,322,323,324,325,326,
327,328,329,330,331,332,333,334,335,336,337,338,339,340,
341,342,343,344,345,346,347,348,349,350,351,252,353,354,
355,356,357,358,359,360,361,362,363,364,365…

1,2,3,4,5,6,7,8,9,10,11,12,13,14,15,16,17,18,19,20,21,22,23,24,
25,26,27,28,29,30,31,32,33,34,35,36,37,38,39,40,41,42,43,44,
45,46,47,48,49,50,51,52,53,54,55,56,57,58,59,60,61,62,63,64,
65,66,67,68,69,70,71,72,73,74,75,76,77,78,79,80,81,82,83,84
,85,86,87,88,89,90,91,92,93,94,95,95,96,97,98,99,100,101,102,
103,104,105,106,107,108,109,110,111,112,113,114,115,116,
117,118,119,120,121,122,123,124,125,126,127,128,129,130,
131,132,133,134,135,136,137,138,139,140,141,142,143,144,
145,146,147,148,149,150,151,152,153,154,155,156,157,158,
159,160,161,162,163,164,165,166,167,168,169,170,171,172,
173,174,175,176,177,178,179,180,181,182,183,184,185,186,
187,188,189,190,191,192,193,194,195,196,197,198,199,200,
201,202,203,204,205,206,207,208,209,210,211,212,213,214,
215,216,217,218,219,220,221,222,223,224,225,226,227,228,
229,230,231,232,233,234,235,236,237,238,239,240,241,242,
243,244,245,246,247,248,249,250,251,252,253,254,255,256,
257,258,259,260,261,262,263,264,265,266,267,268,269,270,
271,272,273,274,275,276,277,278,279,280,281,282,283,284,
285,286,287,288,289,290,291,292,293,294,295,296,297,298,
299,300,301,302,303,304,305,306,307,308,309,310,311,312,
313,314,315,316,317,318,319,320,321,322,323,324,325,326,
327,328,329,330,331,332,333,334,335,336,337,338,339,340,
341,342,343,344,345,346,347,348,349,350,351,252,353,354,
355,356,357,358,359,360,361,362,363,364,365…

1,2,3,4,5,6,7,8,9,10,11,12,13,14,15,16,17,18,19,20,21,22,23,24,

25,26,27,28,29,30,31,32,33,34,35,36,37,38,39,40,41,42,43,44,
45,46,47,48,49,50,51,52,53,54,55,56,57,58,59,60,61,62,63,64,
65,66,67,68,69,70,71,72,73,74,75,76,77,78,79,80,81,82,83,84
,85,86,87,88,89,90,91,92,93,94,95,95,96,97,98,99,100,101,102,
103,104,105,106,107,108,109,110,111,112,113,114,115,116,
117,118,119,120,121,122,123,124,125,126,127,128,129,130,
131,132,133,134,135,136,137,138,139,140,141,142,143,144,
145,146,147,148,149,150,151,152,153,154,155,156,157,158,
159,160,161,162,163,164,165,166,167,168,169,170,171,172,
173,174,175,176,177,178,179,180,181,182,183,184,185,186,
187,188,189,190,191,192,193,194,195,196,197,198,199,200,
201,202,203,204,205,206,207,208,209,210,211,212,213,214,
215,216,217,218,219,220,221,222,223,224,225,226,227,228,
229,230,231,232,233,234,235,236,237,238,239,240,241,242,
243,244,245,246,247,248,249,250,251,252,253,254,255,256,
257,258,259,260,261,262,263,264,265,266,267,268,269,270,
271,272,273,274,275,276,277,278,279,280,281,282,283,284,
285,286,287,288,289,290,291,292,293,294,295,296,297,298,
299,300,301,302,303,304,305,306,307,308,309,310,311,312,
313,314,315,316,317,318,319,320,321,322,323,324,325,326,
327,328,329,330,331,332,333,334,335,336,337,338,339,340,
341,342,343,344,345,346,347,348,349,350,351,252,353,354,
355,356,357,358,359,360,361,362,363,364,365…

1,2,3,4,5,6,7,8,9,10,11,12,13,14,15,16,17,18,19,20,21,22,23,24,
25,26,27,28,29,30,31,32,33,34,35,36,37,38,39,40,41,42,43,44,
45,46,47,48,49,50,51,52,53,54,55,56,57,58,59,60,61,62,63,64,
65,66,67,68,69,70,71,72,73,74,75,76,77,78,79,80,81,82,83,84
,85,86,87,88,89,90,91,92,93,94,95,95,96,97,98,99,100,101,102,
103,104,105,106,107,108,109,110,111,112,113,114,115,116,
117,118,119,120,121,122,123,124,125,126,127,128,129,130,
131,132,133,134,135,136,137,138,139,140,141,142,143,144,
145,146,147,148,149,150,151,152,153,154,155,156,157,158,
159,160,161,162,163,164,165,166,167,168,169,170,171,172,

173,174,175,176,177,178,179,180,181,182,183,184,185,186,
187,188,189,190,191,192,193,194,195,196,197,198,199,200,
201,202,203,204,205,206,207,208,209,210,211,212,213,214,
215,216,217,218,219,220,221,222,223,224,225,226,227,228,
229,230,231,232,233,234,235,236,237,238,239,240,241,242,
243,244,245,246,247,248,249,250,251,252,253,254,255,256,
257,258,259,260,261,262,263,264,265,266,267,268,269,270,
271,272,273,274,275,276,277,278,279,280,281,282,283,284,
285,286,287,288,289,290,291,292,293,294,295,296,297,298,
299,300,301,302,303,304,305,306,307,308,309,310,311,312,
313,314,315,316,317,318,319,320,321,322,323,324,325,326,
327,328,329,330,331,332,333,334,335,336,337,338,339,340,
341,342,343,344,345,346,347,348,349,350,351,252,353,354,
355,356,357,358,359,360,361,362,363,364,365…

1,2,3,4,5,6,7,8,9,10,11,12,13,14,15,16,17,18,19,20,21,22,23,24,
25,26,27,28,29,30,31,32,33,34,35,36,37,38,39,40,41,42,43,44,
45,46,47,48,49,50,51,52,53,54,55,56,57,58,59,60,61,62,63,64,
65,66,67,68,69,70,71,72,73,74,75,76,77,78,79,80,81,82,83,84
,85,86,87,88,89,90,91,92,93,94,95,95,96,97,98,99,100,101,102,
103,104,105,106,107,108,109,110,111,112,113,114,115,116,
117,118,119,120,121,122,123,124,125,126,127,128,129,130,
131,132,133,134,135,136,137,138,139,140,141,142,143,144,
145,146,147,148,149,150,151,152,153,154,155,156,157,158,
159,160,161,162,163,164,165,166,167,168,169,170,171,172,
173,174,175,176,177,178,179,180,181,182,183,184,185,186,
187,188,189,190,191,192,193,194,195,196,197,198,199,200,
201,202,203,204,205,206,207,208,209,210,211,212,213,214,
215,216,217,218,219,220,221,222,223,224,225,226,227,228,
229,230,231,232,233,234,235,236,237,238,239,240,241,242,
243,244,245,246,247,248,249,250,251,252,253,254,255,256,
257,258,259,260,261,262,263,264,265,266,267,268,269,270,
271,272,273,274,275,276,277,278,279,280,281,282,283,284,
285,286,287,288,289,290,291,292,293,294,295,296,297,298,

299,300,301,302,303,304,305,306,307,308,309,310,311,312,
313,314,315,316,317,318,319,320,321,322,323,324,325,326,
327,328,329,330,331,332,333,334,335,336,337,338,339,340,
341,342,343,344,345,346,347,348,349,350,351,252,353,354,
355,356,357,358,359,360,361,362,363,364,365…

1,2,3,4,5,6,7,8,9,10,11,12,13,14,15,16,17,18,19,20,21,22,23,24,
25,26,27,28,29,30,31,32,33,34,35,36,37,38,39,40,41,42,43,44,
45,46,47,48,49,50,51,52,53,54,55,56,57,58,59,60,61,62,63,64,
65,66,67,68,69,70,71,72,73,74,75,76,77,78,79,80,81,82,83,84
,85,86,87,88,89,90,91,92,93,94,95,95,96,97,98,99,100,101,102,
103,104,105,106,107,108,109,110,111,112,113,114,115,116,
117,118,119,120,121,122,123,124,125,126,127,128,129,130,
131,132,133,134,135,136,137,138,139,140,141,142,143,144,
145,146,147,148,149,150,151,152,153,154,155,156,157,158,
159,160,161,162,163,164,165,166,167,168,169,170,171,172,
173,174,175,176,177,178,179,180,181,182,183,184,185,186,
187,188,189,190,191,192,193,194,195,196,197,198,199,200,
201,202,203,204,205,206,207,208,209,210,211,212,213,214,
215,216,217,218,219,220,221,222,223,224,225,226,227,228,
229,230,231,232,233,234,235,236,237,238,239,240,241,242,
243,244,245,246,247,248,249,250,251,252,253,254,255,256,
257,258,259,260,261,262,263,264,265,266,267,268,269,270,
271,272,273,274,275,276,277,278,279,280,281,282,283,284,
285,286,287,288,289,290,291,292,293,294,295,296,297,298,
299,300,301,302,303,304,305,306,307,308,309,310,311,312,
313,314,315,316,317,318,319,320,321,322,323,324,325,326,
327,328,329,330,331,332,333,334,335,336,337,338,339,340,
341,342,343,344,345,346,347,348,349,350,351,252,353,354,
355,356,357,358,359,360,361,362,363,364,365…

1,2,3,4,5,6,7,8,9,10,11,12,13,14,15,16,17,18,19,20,21,22,23,24,
25,26,27,28,29,30,31,32,33,34,35,36,37,38,39,40,41,42,43,44,
45,46,47,48,49,50,51,52,53,54,55,56,57,58,59,60,61,62,63,64,

65,66,67,68,69,70,71,72,73,74,75,76,77,78,79,80,81,82,83,84
,85,86,87,88,89,90,91,92,93,94,95,95,96,97,98,99,100,101,102,
103,104,105,106,107,108,109,110,111,112,113,114,115,116,
117,118,119,120,121,122,123,124,125,126,127,128,129,130,
131,132,133,134,135,136,137,138,139,140,141,142,143,144,
145,146,147,148,149,150,151,152,153,154,155,156,157,158,
159,160,161,162,163,164,165,166,167,168,169,170,171,172,
173,174,175,176,177,178,179,180,181,182,183,184,185,186,
187,188,189,190,191,192,193,194,195,196,197,198,199,200,
201,202,203,204,205,206,207,208,209,210,211,212,213,214,
215,216,217,218,219,220,221,222,223,224,225,226,227,228,
229,230,231,232,233,234,235,236,237,238,239,240,241,242,
243,244,245,246,247,248,249,250,251,252,253,254,255,256,
257,258,259,260,261,262,263,264,265,266,267,268,269,270,
271,272,273,274,275,276,277,278,279,280,281,282,283,284,
285,286,287,288,289,290,291,292,293,294,295,296,297,298,
299,300,301,302,303,304,305,306,307,308,309,310,311,312,
313,314,315,316,317,318,319,320,321,322,323,324,325,326,
327,328,329,330,331,332,333,334,335,336,337,338,339,340,
341,342,343,344,345,346,347,348,349,350,351,252,353,354,
355,356,357,358,359,360,361,362,363,364,365…

1,2,3,4,5,6,7,8,9,10,11,12,13,14,15,16,17,18,19,20,21,22,23,24,
25,26,27,28,29,30,31,32,33,34,35,36,37,38,39,40,41,42,43,44,
45,46,47,48,49,50,51,52,53,54,55,56,57,58,59,60,61,62,63,64,
65,66,67,68,69,70,71,72,73,74,75,76,77,78,79,80,81,82,83,84
,85,86,87,88,89,90,91,92,93,94,95,95,96,97,98,99,100,101,102,
103,104,105,106,107,108,109,110,111,112,113,114,115,116,
117,118,119,120,121,122,123,124,125,126,127,128,129,130,
131,132,133,134,135,136,137,138,139,140,141,142,143,144,
145,146,147,148,149,150,151,152,153,154,155,156,157,158,
159,160,161,162,163,164,165,166,167,168,169,170,171,172,
173,174,175,176,177,178,179,180,181,182,183,184,185,186,
187,188,189,190,191,192,193,194,195,196,197,198,199,200,

201,202,203,204,205,206,207,208,209,210,211,212,213,214,
215,216,217,218,219,220,221,222,223,224,225,226,227,228,
229,230,231,232,233,234,235,236,237,238,239,240,241,242,
243,244,245,246,247,248,249,250,251,252,253,254,255,256,
257,258,259,260,261,262,263,264,265,266,267,268,269,270,
271,272,273,274,275,276,277,278,279,280,281,282,283,284,
285,286,287,288,289,290,291,292,293,294,295,296,297,298,
299,300,301,302,303,304,305,306,307,308,309,310,311,312,
313,314,315,316,317,318,319,320,321,322,323,324,325,326,
327,328,329,330,331,332,333,334,335,336,337,338,339,340,
341,342,343,344,345,346,347,348,349,350,351,252,353,354,
355,356,357,358,359,360,361,362,363,364,365…

1,2,3,4,5,6,7,8,9,10,11,12,13,14,15,16,17,18,19,20,21,22,23,24,
25,26,27,28,29,30,31,32,33,34,35,36,37,38,39,40,41,42,43,44,
45,46,47,48,49,50,51,52,53,54,55,56,57,58,59,60,61,62,63,64,
65,66,67,68,69,70,71,72,73,74,75,76,77,78,79,80,81,82,83,84
,85,86,87,88,89,90,91,92,93,94,95,95,96,97,98,99,100,101,102,
103,104,105,106,107,108,109,110,111,112,113,114,115,116,
117,118,119,120,121,122,123,124,125,126,127,128,129,130,
131,132,133,134,135,136,137,138,139,140,141,142,143,144,
145,146,147,148,149,150,151,152,153,154,155,156,157,158,
159,160,161,162,163,164,165,166,167,168,169,170,171,172,
173,174,175,176,177,178,179,180,181,182,183,184,185,186,
187,188,189,190,191,192,193,194,195,196,197,198,199,200,
201,202,203,204,205,206,207,208,209,210,211,212,213,214,
215,216,217,218,219,220,221,222,223,224,225,226,227,228,
229,230,231,232,233,234,235,236,237,238,239,240,241,242,
243,244,245,246,247,248,249,250,251,252,253,254,255,256,
257,258,259,260,261,262,263,264,265,266,267,268,269,270,
271,272,273,274,275,276,277,278,279,280,281,282,283,284,
285,286,287,288,289,290,291,292,293,294,295,296,297,298,
299,300,301,302,303,304,305,306,307,308,309,310,311,312,
313,314,315,316,317,318,319,320,321,322,323,324,325,326,

327,328,329,330,331,332,333,334,335,336,337,338,339,340,
341,342,343,344,345,346,347,348,349,350,351,252,353,354,
355,356,357,358,359,360,361,362,363,364,365…

1,2,3,4,5,6,7,8,9,10,11,12,13,14,15,16,17,18,19,20,21,22,23,24,
25,26,27,28,29,30,31,32,33,34,35,36,37,38,39,40,41,42,43,44,
45,46,47,48,49,50,51,52,53,54,55,56,57,58,59,60,61,62,63,64,
65,66,67,68,69,70,71,72,73,74,75,76,77,78,79,80,81,82,83,84
,85,86,87,88,89,90,91,92,93,94,95,95,96,97,98,99,100,101,102,
103,104,105,106,107,108,109,110,111,112,113,114,115,116,
117,118,119,120,121,122,123,124,125,126,127,128,129,130,
131,132,133,134,135,136,137,138,139,140,141,142,143,144,
145,146,147,148,149,150,151,152,153,154,155,156,157,158,
159,160,161,162,163,164,165,166,167,168,169,170,171,172,
173,174,175,176,177,178,179,180,181,182,183,184,185,186,
187,188,189,190,191,192,193,194,195,196,197,198,199,200,
201,202,203,204,205,206,207,208,209,210,211,212,213,214,
215,216,217,218,219,220,221,222,223,224,225,226,227,228,
229,230,231,232,233,234,235,236,237,238,239,240,241,242,
243,244,245,246,247,248,249,250,251,252,253,254,255,256,
257,258,259,260,261,262,263,264,265,266,267,268,269,270,
271,272,273,274,275,276,277,278,279,280,281,282,283,284,
285,286,287,288,289,290,291,292,293,294,295,296,297,298,
299,300,301,302,303,304,305,306,307,308,309,310,311,312,
313,314,315,316,317,318,319,320,321,322,323,324,325,326,
327,328,329,330,331,332,333,334,335,336,337,338,339,340,
341,342,343,344,345,346,347,348,349,350,351,252,353,354,
355,356,357,358,359,360,361,362,363,364,365…

1,2,3,4,5,6,7,8,9,10,11,12,13,14,15,16,17,18,19,20,21,22,23,24,
25,26,27,28,29,30,31,32,33,34,35,36,37,38,39,40,41,42,43,44,
45,46,47,48,49,50,51,52,53,54,55,56,57,58,59,60,61,62,63,64,
65,66,67,68,69,70,71,72,73,74,75,76,77,78,79,80,81,82,83,84
,85,86,87,88,89,90,91,92,93,94,95,95,96,97,98,99,100,101,102,

103,104,105,106,107,108,109,110,111,112,113,114,115,116,
117,118,119,120,121,122,123,124,125,126,127,128,129,130,
131,132,133,134,135,136,137,138,139,140,141,142,143,144,
145,146,147,148,149,150,151,152,153,154,155,156,157,158,
159,160,161,162,163,164,165,166,167,168,169,170,171,172,
173,174,175,176,177,178,179,180,181,182,183,184,185,186,
187,188,189,190,191,192,193,194,195,196,197,198,199,200,
201,202,203,204,205,206,207,208,209,210,211,212,213,214,
215,216,217,218,219,220,221,222,223,224,225,226,227,228,
229,230,231,232,233,234,235,236,237,238,239,240,241,242,
243,244,245,246,247,248,249,250,251,252,253,254,255,256,
257,258,259,260,261,262,263,264,265,266,267,268,269,270,
271,272,273,274,275,276,277,278,279,280,281,282,283,284,
285,286,287,288,289,290,291,292,293,294,295,296,297,298,
299,300,301,302,303,304,305,306,307,308,309,310,311,312,
313,314,315,316,317,318,319,320,321,322,323,324,325,326,
327,328,329,330,331,332,333,334,335,336,337,338,339,340,
341,342,343,344,345,346,347,348,349,350,351,252,353,354,
355,356,357,358,359,360,361,362,363,364,365…

1,2,3,4,5,6,7,8,9,10,11,12,13,14,15,16,17,18,19,20,21,22,23,24,
25,26,27,28,29,30,31,32,33,34,35,36,37,38,39,40,41,42,43,44,
45,46,47,48,49,50,51,52,53,54,55,56,57,58,59,60,61,62,63,64,
65,66,67,68,69,70,71,72,73,74,75,76,77,78,79,80,81,82,83,84
,85,86,87,88,89,90,91,92,93,94,95,95,96,97,98,99,100,101,102,
103,104,105,106,107,108,109,110,111,112,113,114,115,116,
117,118,119,120,121,122,123,124,125,126,127,128,129,130,
131,132,133,134,135,136,137,138,139,140,141,142,143,144,
145,146,147,148,149,150,151,152,153,154,155,156,157,158,
159,160,161,162,163,164,165,166,167,168,169,170,171,172,
173,174,175,176,177,178,179,180,181,182,183,184,185,186,
187,188,189,190,191,192,193,194,195,196,197,198,199,200,
201,202,203,204,205,206,207,208,209,210,211,212,213,214,
215,216,217,218,219,220,221,222,223,224,225,226,227,228,

229,230,231,232,233,234,235,236,237,238,239,240,241,242,
243,244,245,246,247,248,249,250,251,252,253,254,255,256,
257,258,259,260,261,262,263,264,265,266,267,268,269,270,
271,272,273,274,275,276,277,278,279,280,281,282,283,284,
285,286,287,288,289,290,291,292,293,294,295,296,297,298,
299,300,301,302,303,304,305,306,307,308,309,310,311,312,
313,314,315,316,317,318,319,320,321,322,323,324,325,326,
327,328,329,330,331,332,333,334,335,336,337,338,339,340,
341,342,343,344,345,346,347,348,349,350,351,252,353,354,
355,356,357,358,359,360,361,362,363,364,365…

1,2,3,4,5,6,7,8,9,10,11,12,13,14,15,16,17,18,19,20,21,22,23,24,
25,26,27,28,29,30,31,32,33,34,35,36,37,38,39,40,41,42,43,44,
45,46,47,48,49,50,51,52,53,54,55,56,57,58,59,60,61,62,63,64,
65,66,67,68,69,70,71,72,73,74,75,76,77,78,79,80,81,82,83,84
,85,86,87,88,89,90,91,92,93,94,95,95,96,97,98,99,100,101,102,
103,104,105,106,107,108,109,110,111,112,113,114,115,116,
117,118,119,120,121,122,123,124,125,126,127,128,129,130,
131,132,133,134,135,136,137,138,139,140,141,142,143,144,
145,146,147,148,149,150,151,152,153,154,155,156,157,158,
159,160,161,162,163,164,165,166,167,168,169,170,171,172,
173,174,175,176,177,178,179,180,181,182,183,184,185,186,
187,188,189,190,191,192,193,194,195,196,197,198,199,200,
201,202,203,204,205,206,207,208,209,210,211,212,213,214,
215,216,217,218,219,220,221,222,223,224,225,226,227,228,
229,230,231,232,233,234,235,236,237,238,239,240,241,242,
243,244,245,246,247,248,249,250,251,252,253,254,255,256,
257,258,259,260,261,262,263,264,265,266,267,268,269,270,
271,272,273,274,275,276,277,278,279,280,281,282,283,284,
285,286,287,288,289,290,291,292,293,294,295,296,297,298,
299,300,301,302,303,304,305,306,307,308,309,310,311,312,
313,314,315,316,317,318,319,320,321,322,323,324,325,326,
327,328,329,330,331,332,333,334,335,336,337,338,339,340,
341,342,343,344,345,346,347,348,349,350,351,252,353,354,
355,356,357,358,359,360,361,362,363,364,365…

The 5,110 days
of fourteen years
Corey Wise,
aged 16,
of the "The Central Park Five,"
spent in prison for
an alleged rape
in New York City,
that he
did not commit.

First Taste of Anti-Semitism

As a high school student,
Adam Rubenstein.
worked as a weekend shoes salesman

He won a company trip to London for a week.
The 18 year old bumped into some
English ladies who recognized
a Yank bloke and said "Take us to the Pub."
The ladies were attracted to Adam's
Paul Newman blue eyes.

Adam bought rounds of drinks for the ladies,
and one asked him what his name was.
"My name is Adam Rubenstein."

The ladies excused themselves to the bathroom,
only to never return.
The smarting young man called home,
and before Adam could say a word,
Father Rubenstein said,
"Let me guess, you just had
your first taste of antisemitism."

"Dad, how did you know?"

"Son, antisemitism in England goes back
to the days of William the Conqueror.
Buck up and
enjoy the rest of your trip.

Cheers!"

Confession 66

Computer Dating

In the
course of
my computer
dating days,
if I found out
the woman was

a smoker,

a Republican or

a Dallas Cowboy fan,

she was
disqualified
from
dating
me.

Diner Hipsters

The high school ladies
with purple hair were
escorted to their table
by the Diner Hostess.

The girls sat down,
looked at the menus and
then at their cell phones
before and after
placing their order with the waitress
and while they
consumed their lunch.

They looked at their cell phones
while they waited for their check
and only stopped looking at the cell phones
when they donned their jackets
and left a tip on the table.

As the Diner hipsters
exited the Diner,
one said to the other,
"Good talk!"

The Boing Sandwich

As a seventh grader,
on a Saturday at noontime
I construct a sandwich of
two slices of bread,
mayo,
ham, cheese and
a slice of lettuce.

I bite into
the sandwich and –

BOING!

A rubber biscuit
the sandwich
turns out to be.

That day I
learned the
texture difference
between
lettuce
and a
leaf of
cabbage.

Zip – Zip – Zip

Attending Union Terrace Elementary
in the first half of the 1970's,
I am dancing to the song" One"
by Three Dog Night a
at my 2nd grade Halloween celebration,

I could make my teacher Ms. Sotak laugh and laugh.
It felt good as a 7 year old to have some power
over an adult who graded my
math, language skills and classroom behavior
four times a year.

One day in the hallway on the way to the cafeteria,
I kept hearing this whisper of a sound
"zip, zip, zip, zip" as Ms. Sotak
escorted her 2nd grade class down to the cafeteria.
I could never figure out where the sound came from.

In 2019 as a teacher in my 19th year
as I walk down the hallway of METS Charter School
Jersey City Campus, I hear the
whisper of the "zip, zip, zip, zip."
I am brought back to the hallways of elementary school
boy days and REALIZE the whisper
is coming from between my thighs in my corduroy pants
rubbing against each other.

I will join Weight Watchers or become
the next victim of spontaneous combustion.

Never Again (2001)

After a Friday night
at the NYC bar
with my
teaching peers,
I think,
"I can drink one more
with no ill effects."

It never seems
to be
heavy drinking
in the moment
until the bed
starts spinning
like the Tilt-a-whirl
at Dorney Park.

Hugging the bowl
making noises such as
"Eh, wretch, sploosh,
blech, blargh and eerk!"
Never again!
NEVER AGAIN!

Until the poison of
the snake bite has
worn off
and the next evening of
"Eh, wretch, sploosh,
Blech, blargh and eerk"
and I repeat
"Never again!"

Prank Names #6

Anna Graham

Chris P. Nugget

Dinah Sore

Eve Ning

Herb E. Side

Kerry O'Seen

Sara Tonin

Phil McCrackin

Travis Tay

Walter Mellon

Made in the USA
Middletown, DE
26 August 2020